For Richard,
in friendship in the art
Al Hirschfeld

THE OCTOBER PALACE

Books by Jane Hirshfield

Poetry
The October Palace
Of Gravity & Angels
Alaya

Anthology
Women in Praise of the Sacred
43 Centuries of Spiritual Poetry by Women

Translation
The Ink Dark Moon (with Mariko Aratani)

THE OCTOBER PALACE

Poems by

Jane Hirshfield

HarperPerennial

A Division of HarperCollins*Publishers*

HarperCollins books may be purchased for educational, business, or sales promotional use. For information please write: Special Markets Department, HarperCollins Publishers, Inc., 10 East 53rd Street, New York, NY 10022.

FIRST EDITION

Designed and Produced by David Bullen

The author wishes to acknowledge gratefully the periodicals in which many of these poems first appeared: *American Poetry Review:* "Inspiration," "This Love," "Under the River," "An Earthly Beauty," "The Gods Are Not Large"; *Antaeus:* "Cycladic Figure: The Harp Player (ca. 3000 B.C.E.)"; *The Atlantic Monthly:* "The Love of Aged Horses," "Within This Tree"; *The Bloomsbury Review:* "The Door"; *Colorado Review:* "At the Roosevelt Baths," "In the Year Eight Hundred," "The Sting"; *Denver Quarterly:* "A Plenitude," "The World"; *Green:* "The November Angels," "What the Heart Wants"; *Manoa:* "A Breakable Spell," "Happiness," "A Recurring Possibility"; *The Midnight Lamp:* "Just Below the Surface," "Leaving the October Palace"; *The Missouri Review:* "What Falls"; *The Nation:* "History as the Painter Bonnard," "Red Poppies"; *New Letters:* "The Ritual," "The Water Diamonds"; *Paris Review:* "Autumn," "The Heart as Origami," "The Mesmer," "The Stone of Heaven," "The Wedding," "The Weighing"; *Ploughshares:* "At Nightfall," "The Window"; *The Plum Review:* "Each Step," "Floor," "Of the Body," "'Perceptibility Is a Kind of Attentiveness'"; *Poetry:* "A Sweetening All Around Me as It Falls";
(continued on page 95, which constitutes an extension of copyright page)

Library of Congress Cataloging-in-Publication Data

Hirshfield, Jane, 1953–
    The October palace / Jane Hirshfield.
      p. cm.
    ISBN 0-06-055348-0 / ISBN 0-06-096997-0 (pbk.)
    I. Title.
    PS 3558.I694025 1994   93-21302
    811'.54—dc20

94 95 96 97 98 HC 10 9 8 7 6 5 4 3 2 1

94 95 96 97 98 HC 10 9 8 7 6 5 4 3 2 1 (pbk.)

For Michael

CONTENTS

II. The Answering Yes

III. The October Palace

THE OCTOBER PALACE

THE KINGDOM

At times
the heart
stands back
and looks at the body,
looks at the mind,
as a lion
quietly looks
at the not-quite-itself,
not-quite-another,
moving of shadows and grass.

Wary, but with interest,
considers its kingdom.

Then seeing
all that will be,
heart once again enters—
enters hunger, enters sorrow,
enters finally losing it all.
To know, if nothing else,
what it once owned.

I.

What the Heart Wants

What the Heart Wants

See then
what the heart wants,
that pliable iron
sprung to the poppy's redness,
the honey's gold, winged
as the heron-lit water is:
by reflecting.
As an aged elephant answers
the slightest, first gesture of hand,
it puts itself at the mercy—
utterly docile, the forces
that brought it there vanished,
fold into fold.
And the old-ice ivory, the unstartlable
black of the eye that has travelled so far
with the fringed, peripheral howdah
swaying behind, look mildly back
as it swings the whole bulk of the body
close to the ground. Over and over
it does this, bends to what asks.
Whatever asks, heart kneels and offers to bear.

RED POPPIES

Inside the metal, all things blossom.
Yet how lightly
the carpenters carry their strands of rebar
down the side of the house,
let them spill with the clashing of broken glass.
While coming up,
barrow on barrow of earth and rock, making way.
Soon now the trenches will fill with concrete,
its quiet hardening into Form.
The rough planks there only briefly,
to hold the moment of changing in their arms,
like the old men of Argos, skinny and proud,
who haunt what is left of the Lion-Gate Palace,
conducting its music of slurrying silence and stone.
Here, one of them pointed, and showed me the King's room,
and then the hidden passageway down to the stream,
the steep descent tasting of oceans,
while the one spring opened around it in so many poppies
they could not be named, revealing themselves
in each petal's sexual brightness,
wanting so much to be found, the gold pollen
spun half to thick honey, half into seeds dark as lead.
The same wanting that finds itself here now, humming within us,
carrying hammer or groceries, hiding its wings.
As it hummed to those alchemists, hard at the work
of the Mind but their arms growing tired at the end of the day,
who found themselves suddenly, finally human—
loving the weight of the body, its mercurial bruises,
its confident bone. All that, now it was heavy, they saw
could be lifted—red flower and black seed—for the first time.

Each Step

Nowhere on this earth
is it not a place where the lovers
turn lightly in sleep in each other's arms,
the blue pastures of dusk flowing gladly
into the dawn.

Nowhere that is not reached by the scent
of good bread
through an open window,
by the flash of fish in the flashing of summer streams,
or the trees unfolding their praises—
apricots, pears—of the winter-chill nights.

Briefly, briefly, we see it, and forget.
As if the spell were too powerful to hold on the tongue,
as if we preferred the weight to the prize—

Like a horse
that carries on his own back
the sacks of oats he will need, unsuspecting,
looking always ahead,
over the mountains, to where sweet springs lie.

He remembers this much from his youth,
the taste of things, cold and pure—
while the water-sound sings on and on, unlistened to,
in his ears;
while each step is nothing less than the glistening
river-body reentering home.

THE SHADOW

That morning, sitting quietly,
I knew for a moment
the unlocked transom of the body:
how the rib-staves bridge a sheer lake
the same within them as without;
how the wrist bones spill the sky's austere
unwaking when the crickets have been still
for hours and the wrens' low whistles
and rasp-tongued blue jays have not yet begun.
Across the continent it was full light,
and a man I loved was tending the body of his mother.
Not the one already ash, but the one of paper,
slipped into drawers, packed into trunks, left behind.
His fingers were turning the smoothed-flat pages,
the middles' ink-dark thicket to be passed through
as the black scribblings of birth-ink and death-ink
must be passed through, and the edges white because the body
has its limits, there are things unspoken between mothers
and sons, and when he tried to tell me,
later, what it was like, there were silences too,
between us and within us. Listen, he said then,
and I did, while he held the receiver's open mouthpiece
toward the east. In each of our bodies, the sea
swung close, then farther off, on its watery stem.
By then, it was night again for us both, another day paid out
in bolted cloth. "Memory," she'd once written, "is like the shadow
of a building, longest just when it turns to disappear. . . ."
Still we stayed on the open phone line hearing
the beating, breaking, scoured-out chimes of wave-scrub—
diamond and black the space between them, empty, vast,
I almost could see it—for a long silent time, remembering her.

THE HOUSE IN WINTER

Here,
in the year's late tidewash,
a corner cupboard suddenly wavers
in low-flung sunlight,
cupboard never quite visible before.

Its jars
of last summer's peaches
have come into their native gold—
not the sweetness of last summer,
but today's,
fresh from the tree of winter.
The mouth swallows *peach*, and says *gold*.

Though they dazzle and are gone,
the halves of fruit, the winter light,
the cupboard it has swept back into shadow.

As inhaled swiftly or slowly,
the sweet-wood scent goes out the same—
saying, *not world but the bright self breathing;*
saying, *not self but the world's bright breath.*
Saying finally, always, *gone,*
the deep shelves of systole and diastole empty.

Or perhaps it is
that the house only constructs itself
while we look—
opens, room from room, *because* we look.
The wood, the glass, the linen, flinging themselves

into form at the clap of our footsteps.
As the hard-dormant
peach tree wades into blossom and leaf
at the spring sun's knock: neither surprised
nor expectant, but every cell awakened at that knock.

CYCLADIC FIGURE:
THE HARP PLAYER (ca. 3000 B.C.E.)

Body out of whose being
Orpheus stepped,
already you
were a whole, already
you had become perfection.
Your face is tipped
upward in simple, oval listening,
as all of your kind's
were tipped upward—
like a blind cup to the blind sun,
yet something
passing between them.
Your hands are unmoving,
the harp's white triangle
balances empty above your thighs,
it is the same
substance as the thighs,
it is the thighs' singing, shown.
We have grown more modest:
singing comes now through the ears,
the head bends downward
in concentration,
like pendulous flowers' heads
from long standing in rain,
or perhaps from the weight
of too much seeing, too much seen.
Your marble is
flawless, continuous, seamless.
When I look at you
you do not look back,

your only direction is inner,
everything enters.
And so the Other
had to step out of you,
into desire,
into Orpheus and incompletion.
The earth—
how could you know this,
who had no ears, who had no eyes?—
wanting so much to be heard,
even the broken-tongued grieving,
that instant clamor,
seemed to it plausible, lovely.

HISTORY AS THE PAINTER BONNARD

Because nothing is ever finished
the painter would shuffle, *bonnarding*,
into galleries, museums, even the homes of his patrons,
with hidden palette and brush:
overscribble drapery and table with milk jug or fattened pear,
the clabbered, ripening colors of second sight.

Though he knew with time the pentimenti rise—
half-visible, half brine-swept fish, their plunged shapes
pocking the mind—toward the end, only revision mattered:
to look again, more deeply, harder, clearer,
the one redemption granted us to ask.

This, we say, is what we meant to say. This. This.
—as the kiss, the sorrowful murmur,
may cover a child's bruises, if not retract the blow.
While a woman in Prague asks softly, in good English
for the camera, "But who will give us back these twenty years?"

Ah love, o history, forgive
the squandered light and flung-down rags of chances,
old choices drifted terribly awry.
And world, self-portrait never right, receive this gift—
shuffling, spattered, stubborn,
something nameless opens in the heart: to touch
with soft-bent sable, ground-earth pigment, seed-clear oil,
the rounding, bright-fleshed present, if not the past.

The kissed child puts his hand at last back into his mother's,
though it is not the same;
her fine face neither right nor wrong, only thoroughly his.

(November–December 1989)

THE WEDDING

Nothing is lost, nothing created: everything is transformed.
Antoine Laurent Lavoisier, *Elements of Chemistry*, 1789

The high windows stream with fish,
the gold luck of carp,
the tiny silver luck of minnows,
while the earth gives back her buried wealth
of skunks and star-crossed badgers:
pure stripes of seeing unfurl themselves
out of moonlight, and the dark bodies
follow as closely as boat follows sail
and know no harm will come to them in their wholeness.
All beings rise, uncaught, for this beginning.
Cousin Death joins a table at the wedding,
the white cloth gleams, the waiting plates,
all are made welcome.
Mother War smooths the silk of her dress,
she feels young and will dance again, after years,
with her husband, Pity.
Still the guests are arriving, carrying gifts:
small appliances, vases, a thick set of towels,
lamps of heaviest brass.
They say each other's names, Charity, Hope, and ask
of nieces and nephews off to school.
A rabbit edges near, outside the glass.
On the river a barge floats softly, its tugs at slack;
night herons and pelicans preen, an iron bell warms
with the slow ringing fire of rust and the barge imperceptibly
lowers. Imagine nothing created, what it might look like,
try to envision such peace.
Now see the dark-shelled flowers of thought unmade,
the petals of Little Boy unassembled,
the plague-poxed donkeys unflung over city walls, the dead

undead, the survivors unlonely. Or think of a world
in which nothing is lost, its heaped paintings,
the studded statues keeping their jewels.
Now see this very world, where all is transformed,
quick as a child who cries and then laughs in her crying—
now ingot, now blossoming ash,
now table, now suckling lamb on that table.
How each thing meets the other as itself, the luminous, changing
mirror of itself—mercuric oxide tipped from flask to flask,
first two, then one, wedded for life in that vow.

A PLENITUDE

Even from a book of aging plates
these frescoes' intricate traceries
dazzle the eye
with their crazed-china, fourteenth-century glaze:
in gold walls, gold vines
flicker and rise in intertwining diamonds,
in red bedding, damask blooms—
Each swath of floor or cloth
a plenitude that binds,
each peak-roofed canopy
a worked geometry of laddered tiles
or stones whose almost-symmetry is repetition
as in nature, invented always new.
For these storied rooms seem not so much
built up by plan as breathed,
until at times they seem to break
as if from sheer exuberance to dapplings
spilled out selfless as animal pelts
or roots whose autumn pattern nets a hill
against the rain's entreating beat to join in falling.
Other times, though,
they seem delicately revealed,
as if some smooth and outer rind had been peeled back
to show the web of sweet-celled seed on seed
that is the world.
But there is the story, too,
of a young painter meeting the envoy of a Pope.
Asked for a work by which his art
could be weighed against others', he dipped his stylus—
with great courtesy, according to Vasari—

in red ink, and drew a single, perfect O.
Shocked, the messenger asked, "Will this be all?"
Young Giotto (whose deerfly his teacher had tried in vain
to brush from a painting) replied,
"It is enough and more."

NARCISSUS: TEL AVIV, BAGHDAD, SAN FRANCISCO; FEBRUARY 1991

And then the precise
opening everywhere of the flowers,
which live after all in their own time.
It seemed they were oblivious but they were not,
they included it all, the nameless explosions
and the oil fires in every cell, the white petals
like mirrors opening in a slow-motion coming-apart
and the stems, the stems rising like green-flaring missiles,
like smoke, like the small sounds shaken
from those who were beaten—like dust from a carpet—
into the wind and the spring-scented rain.
They opened because it was time and they had no choice,
as the children were born in that time and that place
and became what they would without choice, or with only
a little choice, perhaps, for the lucky, the foolish or brave.
But precise and in fact wholly peaceful the flowers opened,
and precise and peaceful the earth: opened because it was asked.
Again and again it was asked and earth opened—
flowered and fell—because what was falling had asked
and could not be refused, as the seabirds that ask the green surface
to open are not refused but are instantly welcomed,
that they may enter and eat—
As soon refuse, battered and soaking, the dark mahogany rain.

FOR THE AUTUMN DEAD: ELECTION DAY, 1984

And those other flowers,
the uncounted, night-blooming cereus—
For what purpose do they offer themselves
unseen, and for one night only, to the dark?
By day, the chronicled world goes on—
In Delhi, six hundred dead, Hindu and Sikh,
in Ethiopia, sixty thousand following drought
across the continent's floor;
while in the mouth of one corpse, sandalwood soaked in ghee
is set aflame and the hourglass, narrow-necked, turns again.
We have watched the bud fatten for centuries:
roses rusty as blood, blood spilled out like roses,
and the hauntingly beautiful names of rivers and deities,
animals, birds, flung down like weeds:
for the right to call a place by one phrase or another,
to tell its history with the shadows
on the right side or the left.
While the rain falls less and less for ten years,
no matter what language we summon it with,
and the spark that consumes the body is set by words,
and all our power for knowing and counting cannot change.
And still we fear silence,
we who made our vows with sentences, so many of them
flowering on the tongue, profligate of seed
as only short-lived things are profligate—

One by one, in abundance or in poverty, we find our way,
and whatever is in us of pity and pride.
And speak to you who come after, to whom we are, perhaps,

the merest trace of sorrow, remnant salt
in the tongue's own flesh.
We who wanted only to die with sweetness in our mouths,
to console the children with that hope.

It is not enough
to see only the beauty,
this light
that pools aluminum
in the winter branches of apple—
it is only a sign
of the tree looking out
from the tree,
of the light looking
back at the light,
the long-celled attention.
The leaves too,
and the fruit, distract
in their sweetness and rustling.
As snow distracts,
covering the tree's looking out
with its own,
and the fragrance of blossoms.
Only stripped
of its multiple selves,
its many fabrics of loveliness,
does the tree's eye
step into a form
we can see with our own,
the black roots twisting down
from the heart,
ours equally whorled,
equally silent,
a flood-swept corridor keeping
no vision but life's—
A mirror looks into a mirror,

colorless, plain,
what flows between them
passes like water through a net.
A dragon-palace, but what dragon?
Its flowing scales of emerald,
emerald water;
its roaring rush,
tide-rush of water;
the treasure—oh even the treasure—
treasure of water.

STORM: YADDO, 1989

The night's stampede of winds
and eerie light is over.
The roads are covered with needles, limbs,
torn after-glitter

of hurricane, earthquake, war.
All night awake behind the leaded glass
of her old room, in her old bed,
I read of Plath—

the final blaze of poems, the icy rages,
the moon-black fear that herded her
to words' Lazarus pages,
swept her to dark water

and white stone. And found her once more netted,
trapped and pinned
just as her butterflies predicted—
within this book. Its bitter end:

her grave unmarked, the headstone stripped.
Not for its sentiment—startling, apt—
the Bhagavad Gita's "Even amidst
fierce flames the golden lotus can be planted"—

but because (not here explained)
women kept coming
to deface her husband's name.
Time does not heal, it takes, the broken-winged,

the stung, the stinging.
Calicoed as cats,
the roads this morning feel
a softer, plainer, falling—rain

heavy and straight
as a hive's hung curtains.
Whose scales, I wondered, waking to that quiet
half hung over from some dream,

are supposed to fall from our seeing?
Fishes'? music's? measure's?
The damaged and damaging heart's?
Another, later, teaching—

"What can pass through the door is not the family treasure."

Pivoting like old watches
on their hidden jewels,
the tall trees out the window turn toward winter.

IN THE YEAR EIGHT HUNDRED

Because of bad weather,
fever,
an unusual number
of fires, the Crown Prince Sawara
was (in the year eight hundred,
and after great debate)
declared Emperor of Japan,
though murdered five years before.

It is said that his spirit
was much appeased
and thereafter the kingdom flourished:
even the silkworms' castings
grew whiter, more strong,
on the mulberry leaves of the new court.
Poems were written,
songs of rejoicing sung,
the proper ceremonies enacted in darkened rooms,

and later, his power secured,
the Great One retired;
in order, it was proclaimed,
to better contemplate the various fates of man.

THE RITUAL

Before,
in the cluttered shop,
I must have missed it,
laid on its ivory side between two labels.
One hand-written, yellowed, the other typed.
Depending on which is right,
he died in 1769 at seventy, or else in 1650,
but they each recite one story:
"Sent from mainland China to Formosa,
   Wu Feng was emissary, interpreter, and friend
   to the island's high mountain tribes.
   Grieved that he could not persuade them
   to end their practice of annual sacrifice,
   he finally—disguised—died as their victim.
   Sorrowed, stunned, the elders cancelled the ritual."
Great-hearted Feng—had he been here to see
the Gate of Heavenly Peace, Tiananmen Square,
shattered last year, what more could he have offered
of compassion? Did the student-scholars know of him,
the ones who, so much younger, gave the same?
Did they use chops like his to sign their names,
an equally brilliant Chinese red surrounding the carved-out absence?
And the elders, these new elders—what of them?

A RECURRING POSSIBILITY

Asked on the icy steps
what she concealed in her mantle,
Elizabeth of Hungary
felt compelled to show her husband
the eggs, bread, and meat.
Instead, white roses,
red—though it was mid-December—
spilled from the heavy cloth.
In this miracle, she is most often painted.
After the Landgrave's death,
her confessor grew more and more strict.
Took from her her four children.
Took from her the happiness of good works.
When she died at twenty-four,
the poor had returned to their hunger,
her back was cobwebbed with scars,
her last word was *Silence.*
What would it be to live fully
in these our bodies? It is almost
eight centuries later, it is raining.
The ordinary roses, whose fragrance is earthly,
like her have nothing to say.

THE WORLD

Half-shop, half-museum, it occupies
one corner of its block
in studied gloom,
closed Tuesdays and Thursdays,
though possibly not in summer
when town fills with those who come
to watch horses run.
A half flight of steps leads first
to the windowed room of painted cupolas,
the copper roosters' and mares' tails
streaming south above their well-imagined barns.
The actual underneath—also rough planking—creaks
and scuffs, snugged tightly for all its noises
to its harbor, but the weather vanes fly
their flags, year after year,
 in steady homeward weatherless migration,
arranged by some vanished clerk's hand.
In the main room, huge, the walls on one side
are lined with crocks, some dated,
some painted with bluish landscapes or flowers;
on the other, the owner's pride, a collection of Hummel.
Between, not-quite-valuable books and maps
flake off their lapsing faith in countries and physics,
paste earrings glisten in '30s arrows of bright disguise,
several hundred antique linens and shoes
display their patent and starched-stiff virtues.
What changes all is encased in a corner, far in back:
a clutter of tiny white horses, sweating, their heads held low;
three ox-drawn carts; the fisherman heading off,
his net slung empty as a blow on his tired left shoulder;
a simple, sleeping cat; and a farmer whose feet

assemble unseen furrows, the water buckets' weight
minutely shifting as he goes.
Though some of them stand opened to reveal:
a mountain landscape perching with saints,
a tree branch naved with interior songbirds.
Worlds within worlds, each of them ivory.
A carp, his entire body's length less than an inch,
fans the whole place with his tail—
under his rivering spell, walking sticks, brides' gowns,
and yellowing tablecloths lacily waver.
A clutch of persimmons quietly ripens within a basket
from quinine whiteness
to whiteness of sweetened snow, while nearby
two ivory children, their appetite plain, quietly wait.
And one bullock stands patiently waiting his harness,
each half-starved rib communicative as braille.
A perfect teaching,
complete and stopped here under glass and wooden rail—
for stories persuade, cajole, tremble the language
to honey that clings to the knife.
But these small figures, precise and homely,
carry a different gloss:
a hard-won sorrow, a hard-worn wonder is this world,
this life, beside the case of scrimshaw and mounted umbrellas,
perfectly scrolled and dry for half a century or more.

FLOOR

The nails, once inset, rise to the surface—
or, more truly perhaps, over years
the boards sink down to meet what holds them.
Worn, yes, but not worn through:
the visible work reveals itself in iron,
to be pounded down again, for what we've declared
the beautiful to be.

The Hawk Cry

I do not know
what brought it to the middle
of the room made warm by the fire
I had lit before breakfast.
The day before it had run, seeing me,
out of my sight, but now even the sharp
involuntary animal-warning I made, seeing it,
did not seem to reach it at all.
Perhaps it was sick, or starving,
trapped in this place for days with nothing to eat
but paper. Perhaps it was simply old.
It lay with its eyes pressed closed
and seemed to concentrate hard on whatever it was.
Not knowing what better to do, I nudged it
gently as I could onto the dustpan;
and once, twice, the eyes opened, then shut back down.
I just took it out, rolled that softly pondering
body into the grass.
A few minutes later watched it move off into the weeds.
All day the world went on about its business.
Squirrels carrying acorns, the two thin cats
at their accustomed hour crossing the wash of the sun.
I read and slept a little, drank more coffee.
Why would a dying mouse—whether it lived or died
it must have been dying, to act as it did—
come out that way into the open?
To borrow a few minutes' life from the woodstove's heat?
To better offer itself to the one it must have known
would take it quickly, surely, for its own purpose?
Or was it a simpler surrender even than that,

almost magnetic, to some incomprehensible trust?
It did not fight at all when I gave it
to the broom's yellow stiffness, or lend its assent.
It simply let what happened happen, and even
watched a little as it did.

The Sting

You can almost feel it,
the weaving
of hidden dimensions
through ours,
where the bottle-green
humming of flies
on their isinglass wings
uncodes itself in our ears
and time flings itself
backward as unthinkingly
as this cow thrusts her head,
tongue extended,
toward the rough itch on her spine.

The tongue just makes it,
intention just touches flesh,
and time-future, assuaged, continues
its trek down the trampled-grass,
cow-fragrant path.

Or perhaps,
in one of those
nine or ten infolded worlds,
when cells
flower and flower
themselves into myriad being,
the long halls
of the body rejoice;
perhaps when they darken
and bruise it is into wine,

or toward the intoxicant
nightfall of stars.

Though even here,
in these unhidden
three and the fourth
made visible only by memory,
it astonishes, life, does it not?
The long legs of the wood wasps
gleam in the sun
like spun-gold.
The sting runs as a child
once ran toward the chill river's
plunge, the senseless, pure shock
of the body singing,
not pleasure, not pain.

AUTUMN

Again the wind
flakes gold-leaf from the trees
and the painting darkens—
as if a thousand penitents
kissed an icon
till it thinned
back to bare wood,
without diminishment.

WHAT FALLS

Today, what falls is wavering
from rain to snow to rain, shifting from sound
to silence and back through moments
when only the breath of invisible waters
beads on the windows and eaves and makes its way down.
It does not want to come into the audible music,
the palace where courtiers walk softly in slippers
across the tiled floors.
It wants us to come out, and can wait.
Old love falls in rope-strands of hair from a barber's apron,
quince blossoms fall while attempting to follow the rising new moon,
mutterings fall from our feet when we walk—
first in the pattered notes of the very young,
tuneless and mild,
later the shuffling speech of the very old:
both aimless and pure in their vision of nowhere to go,
a world which is all destination.
Only between do we walk with determined purpose,
pacing the mapped-out roads of our century's life
as we must, though we are wrong to, and even, sometimes,
know we are wrong: the map incorrect and cruelly drawn,
its colors ugly. . . . Now, as I listen,
the falling has changed from not quite the one,
not quite the other, to fully silent, and snow.
Thought that rises like roses out of the intricate carpets
will quiet like this, its reds and blues
muted to flesh-tones, its stylized thorns undone.
The kingdom will fall to a different ruler,
whose armies will go. The halls of the palace, mutable,
mute, will begin to surrender, wild apples will grow,
while somewhere, softly, plows start up their muzzled groan—

What falls is independent angels, flowers, stones, the fragile
lace of colored light through glass, the body's window.
What falls is also snow and only snow, a cold precipitate of watered air,
but crystalline and visible, as we are.

THE DOOR

A note waterfalls steadily
through us,
just below hearing.

Or this early light
streaming through dusty glass:
what enters, enters like that,
unstoppable gift.

And yet there is also the other,
the breath-space held between any call
and its answer—

In the querying
first scuff of footstep,
the wood owls' repeating,
the two-counting heart:

A little sabbath,
minnow whose brightness silvers past time.

The rest-note,
unwritten,
hinged between worlds,
that precedes change and allows it.

II.

The Answering Yes

1973

That winter we took turns stepping into
the barely started mornings to turn ignitions
until they caught, complaining roughly
of the cold, then ran
back to finish our coffee, cereal, toast,
while, chokes pulled full out,
exhaust poured white across the glass
that kept us warm . . .
We'd named them: Big Mama Tomato, Snooze.
Each was our first, as we
were each other's first, in the farmhouse
for rent for the first time
in forty years surrounded by soybeans.
We'd whited-over the pink room the son
had painted when he returned crazed with Vietnam.
We'd made the man come back for the thin black Lab
left chained in the yard.
The thirteen cats stayed, soon more, all wild.
Our own would come to the window by way of
a three-story oak and moss-shingled porch roof,
to mew us awake and them in every day:
Kesey & Mountain Girl, scrawling their signatures
snow-mornings on the quilt.
We nailed planks from the old barns onto the walls
by our bed, scraped a dozen layers of peeling paper
from the next room—the older they got,
the more lovely. That one we made cheerful yellow,
where I wrote the wildly sad poems of the very young.
When we got to the farm you took a tractor, I loaded
my van with sacks of produce & drove off.
Kip supervised us all: the Peace Corps vet, the kids

just out of school. Picking his peaches that summer
the best work I've done, the closest to Paradise
I've seen, ladder-propped in his trees.
All sold now, gone, his farm, the one we lived at,
the groundfall cider, the cars.
Us too, of course, long shaken free, though
I still cook bluefish the way you taught me, and carrots.
I thought I would love you forever—and, a little, I may,
in the way I still move toward a crate, knees bent,
or reach for a man: as one might stretch
for the three or four fruit that lie in the sun at the top
of the tree; too ripe for any moment but this,
they open their skin at first touch, yielding sweetness,
sweetness and heat, and in me, each time since,
the answering yes.

HAPPINESS

I think it was from the animals
that St. Francis learned
it is possible to cast yourself
on the earth's good mercy and live.
From the wolf who cast off
the deep fierceness of her first heart
and crept into the circle of sunlight
in full wariness and wolf-hunger,
and was fed, and lived; from the birds
who came fearless to him until he
had no choice but return that courage.
Even the least amoeba touched on all sides
by the opulent Other, even the baleened
plankton fully immersed in their fate—
for what else might happiness be
than to be porous, opened, rinsed through
by the beings and things?
Nor could he forget those other companions,
the shifting, ethereal, shapeless:
Hopelessness, Desperateness, Loneliness,
even the fire-tongued Anger—
for they too waited with the patient Lion,
the glossy Rooster, the drowsy Mule, to step
out of the trees' protection and come in.

THIS LOVE

Most lovely of the things I loved and lose: the sunlight;
next, bright stars, the moon,
ripe gourds, the fruit of apple trees, the pears.
Praxilla (fl. 440 B.C.E.)

A lucky woman,
Praxilla, to have tasted
the cucumber missed more severely than gold.
And lucky, whoever learns there is only one loss,
the bracelets glinting heavy and warm on the wrist,
fastened there for the first time
by a lover's hand,
and the lizard-cool fruit growing outside the door,
cobbled and rivered with all the green waters of earth.
Exiles, too, must know something
of how it will be, the ones who say not "I miss Paris"
but "Paris is missing me"—
For it is the other which stays, we who depart,
and any piece of it, even the smallest, would more than suffice.
As lifting a single silk thread, the whole cloth must come,
if the silk is strong.
And this love we bear things—
their coarse hide, the blown chaff of their scent—
this love is strong.

INSPIRATION

Think of those Chinese monks' tales:
years of struggling
in the zendo, then the clink,
while sweeping up, of stone on stone . . .
It's Emily's wisdom: Truth in Circuit lies.
Or see Grant's *Common Birds and How to Know Them*
(New York: Scribner's, 1901):
"The approach must be by detour,
advantage taken of rock, tree, mound, and brush,
but if without success this way, use artifice,
throw off all stealth's appearance, watchfulness,
look guileless, a loiterer, purposeless,
stroll on (not too directly toward the bird),
avoiding any gaze too steadfast;
or failing still in this, give voice to sundry whistles,
chirp: your quarry may stay on to answer."
More briefly, try; but stymied, give it up, do something else.
Leave the untrappable thought, go walking,
ideas buzz the air like flies; return to work,
a fox trots by—not Hughes's sharp-stinking thought-fox
but quite real, outside the window,
with cream-dipped tail and red-fire legs doused watery brown;
emerges from the wood's dark margin, stopping all thinking,
and briefly squats (not fox, but vixen), then moves along
and out of sight. "Enlightenment," wrote one master,
"is an accident, though certain efforts make you accident-prone."
The rest slants fox-like, in and out of stones.

The Love of Aged Horses

Because I know tomorrow
his faithful gelding heart will be broken
when the spotted mare is trailered and driven away,
I come today to take him for a gallop on Diaz ridge.

Returning, he will whinny for his love.
Ancient, spavined,
her white parts red with hill-dust,
her red parts whitened with the same, she never answers.

But today, when I turn him loose at the bent gate
with the taste of chewed oat on his tongue
and the saddle-sweat rinsed off with water,
I know he will canter, however tired,
whinnying wildly up the ridge's near side,
and I know he will find her.

He will be filled with the sureness of horses
whose bellies are grain-filled,
whose long-ribbed loneliness
can be scratched into no-longer-lonely.

His long teeth on her withers,
her rough-coated spots will grow damp and wild.
Her long teeth on his withers,
his oiled-teakwood smoothness will grow damp and wild.
Their shadows' chiasmus will fleck and fill with flies,
the eight marks of their fortune stamp and then cancel the earth.
From ear-flick to tail-switch, they stand in one body.
No luck is as boundless as theirs.

At Nightfall

Like held lanterns, wavering,
almost gone out,
the cows' white faces turn toward me
as their bodies pivot, needles to magnetic north.
Squared off, they still, and stare.
I can barely make out the nostrils' dilation
trying to forage my scent
from the currents of air, or the draped-velvet
black of their coats, its crushed sheen.
As if all the brightness so recently glazing these hills
had gone into them when it went, had burnished
the heavy flanks with the gas-blue flame
whose low hiss is the letting down milk, or had opened
the dewlaps' deep curtains and stepped in behind,
drawing closed the body's opacity after.
Though some small part escapes still,
leaking through as we stand in mutual regard:
two cows, two calves, and a two-legged—
homelier animal, if truth be spoken, even than they.
Each of us pinned on the axis that spins out this dusk
as a pupa spins out her cocoon,
white as the coming-in fog being spun just now by the sea,
or the milk spooling down its long thread
into udders that guard the passage
from all other lifetimes to this. In the true north,
that no iron points to, the first stars scratch into
the compass-glass of the sky. One calf,
grown restless, and pleased enough with this world,
butts the side of his dam. She shifts a little,
addresses me gravely a final question, then moves away—

right, I know, not to trust either me or my kind.
Then the fog reaches this place at the moment of darkness
and even the stars go out, recede to the unfenced field
of the no longer seen. There, an assembly
greets them: the man, met once for an hour,
who gave me the book he was reading;
the wooden recorder sighed into until I was ten,
tucked safely back in its sock of brown felt;
the seven lost watches, three rings, and near them
the rhinestone pin, picked out for a teacher truly loved—
all the hard discarded and easily lost,
the gone to the pastures of gone. In a shadowy line, the cows
enter: first cow, then calf, then second cow,
then second calf, each broad nose following closely
each knotted-rope tail. They pause and gaze, seem content,
then lower their heads to the grass that rises
from under the twinned quarter-moons of their hooves.
The grass grows green and greener: it is full daylight,
the air become warm, and filled with the cloverleaf-traffic of flies.
And though a dog is barking—
the white one, waving the plume of her tail—
the cows do not startle, beyond that now as they are,
so the barking continues, gaily, for a long time,
though growing more faint as I make my way up the side of the hill,
taking the path by foot-feel, leaving the low fog behind, until suddenly
from this side another dog answers,
equally happy but this one freckled half-black, half-white,
with a tobacco-twist of color behind each ear;
answers and comes through the darkness, silencing crickets,
wagging me home, urging me   *faster, forward,*
into the impatient present, its spoked-wheel turnings,
wobblings, desires, where I—she seems quite sure of it—belong.

PERCOLATION

In this rain that keeps us inside,
the frog,
wisest of creatures,
to whom all things come,
is happy, rasping out of himself
the tuneless anthem of Frog.
Further off and more like ourselves
the cows are raising a huddling protest,
a ragtag crowd, that can't get its chanting in time.
Now the crickets,
seeming to welcome the early-come twilight,
come in—of all orchestras, the most plaintive.
Still, in this rain soft as fog
that can only be known to be rain by the windows' streaming,
surely all Being at bottom is happy:
soaked to the bone, sopped at the root,
fenny, seeped through, yielding as coffee grounds
yield to their percolation, blushing, completely seduced,
assenting as they give in to the downrushing water,
the murmur of falling, the fluvial, purling wash
of all the ways matter loves matter,
riding its gravity down, into the body,
rising through cell-strands of xylem, leaflet and lung-flower,
back into air.

THE GROUNDFALL PEAR

It is the one he chooses,
yellow, plump, a little bruised
on one side from falling.
That place he takes first.

AT THE ROOSEVELT BATHS

These women ("tough as old chicken"
they'd say of themselves)
still smile
when they see us come in.

They know what we are,
five women who don't know the score.
("And you," mine will soon ask me,
"you must be a poet?" I'll nod yes mutely—

these old women know.) "Now you undress,"
they tell us, and give us
each sheets, twisting open the valve cocks
and starting the bath.

Soon they are doing their math,
adding, subtracting, swinging cool water into the hot
with a sweeping of hands;
they wrap pillows in worn towelling, stop,

stand by the tubs as we clamber in.
Another towel draped over just under the chin
floats on the small-bubbling water,
smelling of sulfur. Everyone else, I'll later discover,

likewise floats on the salt-suffused mix.
Only I sink to the bottom and stay,
an inadequate fish, being nibbled
by minnows of calcite, magnesium, particled clay.

Though I'm happy enough to sway in this pickling
that prickles us all into dream,
until they return softly clucking
and tucking us back into seam-

less white sheeting and sag-bellied cot.
We're left then to steam the prescribed thirty minutes
in stinging-pore drift as
from snow after sauna or heat after sex.

"Come dress now," she cackles,
my guardian crone, "your friends
are all leaving."
I scurry back into blue jeans,

give thanks much refreshed
in the form of a dollar
slipped into the flat paper cup
magic-markered

"Attendant For Bath."
This I trust is the way that
the angels will be
on the days of our deaths.

Just this friendly, this homely,
with just this having-seen-it-all air—
the smooth and the scabbed, the wrinkled, the lonely,
the hip-boned and flabbed, all put in their care.

They will wrap
us in sheets, immerse us
in bubbling, dark waters,
they will tell us to nap.

And when we awaken, snap,
it will be
into just such a day as today:
filled with the chittering

of children and thunkety tennis balls,
always well hit,
thunkety, thunkety,
clearing the net.

A Breakable Spell

I don't know
with what tongue
to answer
this world's constant question—

whether the tongue
of red enamel, or blue,
whether the tongue
of flowing water, or ice,

or the tongue of mountain,
or the split-songed
tongue that embraces first light.

But it keeps asking
and so I continue,
trying *cucumber,* trying *window,*
trying *egret*—

For a moment
she stands with her
elegant legs
black in the water.
Below her, another looks up.

My love,
there is no sound between them.

Then,
inside apples and subways,

in smokestacks,
in blossoming roses,
the heart's machinery starts up again,
hammering and sawing.

FOR A WEDDING ON MOUNT TAMALPAIS

July,
and the rich apples
once again falling.

You put them to your lips,
as you were meant to,
enter a sweetness
the earth wants to give.

Everything loves this way,
in gold honey,
in gold mountain grass
that carries lightly the shadow of hawks,
the shadow of clouds passing by.

And the dry grasses,
the live oaks and bays,
taste the apples' deep sweetness
because you taste it, as you were meant to,
tasting the life that is yours,

while below, the foghorns bend to their work,
bringing home what is coming home,
blessing what goes.

THE MESMER

These mail-ordered tulips,
shockingly gaudy,
open and close, re-open, re-close,
like a storefront, time after time,
until the noon comes that they open too far and are
suddenly vanished,
a shiver of crayon-yellows and reds, of violet
reaching toward black that wind-drifts away across the lawn:
the just fate of the overambitious.
And yet, haven't we each attempted that trick, desiring
ourselves into wideness, more wideness, until we are lost?
But, being human, return to the gaudy shock of Being
once again fleshed,
the solid bodies—as planets are called—
that consciousness wears. Though so close to the rest
that we envy what seems so restful, the water that stills
when held, streams on when let free, and eventually
sinks so far that it comes into air.
Becoming, we say—of a blouse, new-cut hair, of quantum physics'
particles' waves, or the flutter of scarf into dove. . . .
Its colors mesmerize the long nights, keeping us riveted, world-bound,
whispering, *how is it done?*

UNDER THE RIVER

Under the river of the world, the world.
And beneath that palace, a palace—just the same.
From the quarry ledge, children dive
over and over into blue sky:
it always greets them the same,
laughter, then towels, and going home with watery ears.
It sings to them then for hours, hushing the rest—
family, dinnerware, tires spinning by, all stilled.
Open-winged for those moments between world and world,
the rooms leading one to the next,
each linoleum floor marble-cool,
the ceilings stencilled with water lilies, stars.

COURTSHIP

When men come visiting
my flautist friend in Texas,
her parrot Gay
gives back her half-digested seed in love,
her motherhood-excellence endlessly, flawlessly offered . . .

Mostly, though, the usual performance
works: red-breasted robin
dips and struts into brown-breasted robin's heart,
the cardinal's flashy present is accepted.

In perfection,
curve-billed thrashers mate,
and make billed thrashers.
Gray's thrush produce Gray's thrush,
filling each spring corner with common song.
Just yesterday,
checking two outside lanterns, dark year-long,
I found in each a cozy, well-made cone;
and though in one three tiny eggs remained—
white, lightly drizzled with coffee, all drilled through sadly—
the other was successful, perfectly empty.

Strict measures are the kindest thing
in courtship: each partner's
steps prescribed in proper order,
each answer known before the question's even asked.
And how much of love of life, that steadiest marriage,

is simple species-allegiance: the old wife,
the bliss-shared language?

Though some, in wider wooing, kneel to almost anything,
trying to get it so right it breaks your heart—
a Chevrolet's brake shoes, a basketball hoop's
small o of admiration tended and tended,
past private griefs, fatigue, past boredom's rain-stiffened glove.
The daily faithfulness not even recognized as peacock-brilliant love.

THE WATER DIAMONDS

Inside perfection, continents could hide;
behind its doors,
the fierce worlds turn unseen—
smooth surfaces, the dragonflies' blue glide,
conceal the swift-fleshed trout, the spotted bream.

But flaked from its long bones by charring heat,
translucent-swimming will
becomes opaque:
unspirits itself edible and sweet,
and will not travel more except the lake

of human understanding, human fate—
Who would have chosen burial
so fearful?
Yet waters roughen, winds uprising late,
and deep fish rise to feed, as if some riddle

drew them upward to be solved.
The slipped scales throw
a night-sky's worth of icy stars
across the catch-pans where they slow-revolve,
like half-dazed planets. Not quite caught, or ours,

not quite anyone's at all. . . .
A herd of water diamonds, perhaps,
stalled
a moment, two,
within their thousand lives' recall.

FOR A GELDING

No matter that it has been there
six years—one-fourth of his life—
passing the new fence, he shies.
Or soft clouds of thistle-stands gone
to seed, bright circlets of Queen Anne's Lace—
anything white will do. The grey fox,
all summer collapsing into sharp teeth
and the curved light of bones, is more than enough
to tighten my knees five strides before,
for he is always surprised.
He believes that we cannot know
where it will come from, the lion that hides
its fierce claws within Things, but he knows it is white.
And he may be right: sprayed salt flecks the muzzle
deep in the oats of his green plastic pail,
more stars open each year into his neck's early dusk.
I, too, now wear that warning. And so pray
to the four-legged gods as we trot briskly on,
"Oh, for him, in this temperate climate
so near the sea, again this year let it not snow."
For surely the sight would kill him, everything Lion.
But even home-turned in yellow September,
the warmest month here, it could be waiting—
a styrofoam cup, a dropped visor.
He is prepared, will save both of our lives.
Later, he takes his apple and turns
toward the hill where the others drift slowly higher,
to follow the currents of forage. The one he loved—
Candy, half-white and half-red—has gone on ahead.

THE TASK

It is a simple garment, this slipped-on world.
We wake into it daily—open eyes, braid hair—
a robe unfurled
in rose-silk flowering, then laid bare.

And yes, it is a simple enough task
we've taken on,
though also vast:
from dusk to dawn,

from dawn to dusk, to praise, and not
be blinded by the praising.
To lie like a cat in hot
sun, fur fully blazing,

and dream the mouse;
and to keep too the mouse's patient, waking watch
within the deep rooms of the house,
where the leaf-flocked

sunlight never reaches, but the earth still blooms.

IN YELLOW GRASS

In the yellow grass
each gathers with its own kind—
and the lion-beauty cuts that invisible pen,
the bright wires trampled or leapt.

So, love, it will be with us, both
lion and prey—our mouths so deep in richness
only the wild scent of earth will be left
to tremble, after.

But what if the world's
strict questions were not this
unanswerable yellow, that rampant red,
or the black-hearted, pried-open blue?
If the disciplined welter
were not heady with white-scented bloom?
Would love bend like the tulips then
from its quick-flying carriage?
Would tenderness wring the heart still
of its burdens, leaving only the dark-salted
circles on stone-colored ground?
It is the way humans know—
through the earth, through the things of the earth,
lips stained by what they have tasted,
the sweet sap-run, the tart-rinded fruit.
Leave to dogs and the angels
the music that lies beyond hearing.
Though the infinite palace is infinite, it is precise.

III.

The October Palace

A SWEETENING ALL AROUND ME AS IT FALLS

Even generous August,
only a child's scribblings
on thick black paper, in smudgeable chalk—
even the ripening tomatoes, even the roses,
blowsy, loosing their fragrance of black tea.
A winter light held this morning's apples
as they fell, sweet, streaked by one touch
of the careless brush, appling to earth.
The seeds so deep inside they carry that cold.
Is this why some choose solitude, to rise
that small bit further, unencumbered by love of earth,
as the branches, lighter, kite now a little higher
on gold air? But the apples love earth and falling,
lose themselves in it as much as they can at first touch
and then, with time and rain, at last completely:
to be that bone-like One that shines unleafed in winter rain,
all black and glazed with not the pendant gold of
necklaced summer but the ice-color mirroring starlight
when the earth is empty and dark and knows nothing of apples.
Seed-black of the paper, seed-black of the waiting heart—
December's shine, austere and fragile, carves the visible tree.
But today, cut deep in last plums, in yellow pears,
in second flush of roses, in the warmth of an hour, now late,
as drunk on heat as the girl who long ago vanished into green trees,
fold that loneliness, one moment, two, love, back into your arms.

The November Angels

Late dazzle
of yellow
flooding
the simplified woods,
spare chipping away
of the afternoon-stone
by a small brown finch—
there is little
for them to do,
and so their gossip is
idle, modest:
low-growing,
tiny-white-flowered.

Below,
the Earth-pelt
dapples and flows
with slow bees
that spin
the thick, deep jute
of the gold time's going,
the pollen's
traceless retreat;
kingfishers
enter their kingdom,
their blue crowns on fire,
and feast on
the still-wealthy world.

A single, cold blossom
tumbles, fledged
from the sky's white branch.

And the angels
look on,
observing what falls:
all of it falls.

Their hands hold
no blessings,
no word
for those who walk
in the tall black pines,
who do not
feel themselves falling—
the ones who believe
the loved companion
will hold them forever,
the ones who cross through
alone and ask for no sign.

The afternoon
lengthens, steepens,
flares out—
no matter for them.
It is assenting
that makes them angels,
neither increased
nor decreased
by the clamorous heart:
their only work
to shine back,
however the passing brightness
hurts their eyes.

Of the Body

And what of that other net? The one
we willingly give ourselves to, it is that beautiful—
each knot so carefully made, the curved
plate of the sternum tied to the shape of breath,
the perfect hinge of the knee that opens and closes the earth.
The water of the eye very cold, very clear.
And the sturgeon, the golden carp, how they continue to elude us.
Swim straight through and are instantly gone;
though a shadow flickers, remembering.

THE THIEF

Every fire is stolen.
And so lovers,
after, their arms or thighs touching
lightly, find themselves
even in daylight speaking in whispers.
Not to escape the passionate,
vanquished gods, who, the Greeks told us,
hated our happiness with an inexplicable heat,
but because their tenderness raises
its clear, wild sap in artesian tongues of desire
wedded wholly to jealous time.
For fish, water is endless; for birds, the air.
And our element, endless too.
But who can fin unstoppably in desire,
that lifts and lets go legs, outreaches arms,
quickens and slows even breath? It pins us
to this world we thieve and thieve from, want without pause,
the hunger blossoms first of flower, then snow.
Until the single fragrance spilling and we open
to the dark that comes to take us—embrace
that should be brutal, yet somehow not. No, intimate,
almost a kindness, the quick taking.
And then that too is faithfully stripped from our arms.

Leaving the October Palace

In ancient Japan, *to travel*
meant always away—
toward the capital, one spoke only of return.
As these falling needles and leaves speak of return,
their long labors of green tired finally into gold,
the desire that remembered them into place
prepared at last to let go.
Though not for want of faithfulness—
all that once followed the sun still follows it now,
as it turns away.
The courtiers assemble their carriages, fold up their robes.
By daybreak, the soundless mountains bow under snow.

JUST BELOW THE SURFACE

Just below the surface, fish, still.
In the late afternoon, the sunlight ladders down,
breaking across their bodies' narrow poise.
It is almost a music, the brown unmoving quickness
intersected with gold.
They are, even in sleep, wholly alive and one, a necklace
assembled on thread so fine it is almost surmise.
A first moves, another, and they are gone.
As one lover goes, and, long after, the other;
yet somehow, in another shadow of the same water,
are still there.

RIPENESS

Ripeness is
what falls away with ease.
Not only the heavy apple,
the pear,
but also the dried brown strands
of autumn iris from their core.

To let your body
love this world
that gave itself to your care
in all of its ripeness,
with ease,
and will take itself from you
in equal ripeness and ease,
is also harvest.

And however sharply
you are tested—
this sorrow, that great love—
it too will leave on that clean knife.

THE WEIGHING

The heart's reasons
seen clearly,
even the hardest
will carry
its whip-marks and sadness
and must be forgiven.

As the drought-starved
eland forgives
the drought-starved lion
who finally takes her,
enters willingly then
the life she cannot refuse,
and is lion, is fed,
and does not remember the other.

So few grains of happiness
measured against all the dark
and still the scales balance.

The world asks of us
only the strength we have and we give it.
Then it asks more, and we give it.

MEETING THE LIGHT COMPLETELY

Even the long-beloved
was once
an unrecognized stranger.

Just so,
the chipped lip
of a blue-glazed cup,
blown field
of a yellow curtain,
might also,
flooding and falling,
ruin your heart.

A table painted with roses.
An empty clothesline.

Each time,
the found world surprises—
that is its nature.

And then
what is said by all lovers:
"What fools we were, not to have seen."

THE GODS ARE NOT LARGE

But perhaps
the heart
does not want
to be understood.
Your shadow
falls on its pond
and the small fish
hurry away.
They have
their own lives,
not yours,
which they love.

And if to you
it is anger,
bewilderment,
grief,
to them
it is simply life:
their mouths
open and close,
their gills,
they are fed,
they breathe.

The gods
are not large,
outside us.
They are the fish,
going on
with their own concerns.

The Heart as Origami

Each one has its shape.
For love, two sleeping ducks.
For selfless courage, the war-horse.
For fear of death, the daylily's one-day flower.
More and more creased each year, worn paper thin,
and still it longs for them all.
Not one of the lives of this world the heart does not choose.

AN EARTHLY BEAUTY

Others have described
the metal bull placed over fire,
it singing while the man inside it died.
Which emperor listened, in which country,
doesn't matter, though surely
the thing itself was built by slaves.
An unearthly music, all reports agree.
We—the civilized—hearing this story,
recoil from it in horror: Not us. Not ours.
But why does my heart look back at me,
reproachful? Why does the bull?

WITHIN THIS TREE

Within this tree
another tree
inhabits the same body;
within this stone
another stone rests,
its many shades of grey
the same,
its identical
surface and weight.
And within my body,
another body,
whose history, waiting,
sings: *there is no other body,*
it sings,
there is no other world.

EMPEDOCLES' PHYSICS

In all its parts the deep foul valley trembled so
I thought the universe felt love, which some believe
Has many times returned the world to chaos; here below
And elsewhere in that moment, the ancient cliffsides tumbled.

The Inferno, Canto XII

'Aversion carves the self.'
—A Vedic teaching too, though here
it is Empedocles', who wrote
that Hate creates our fractal'd world,
which Love would have a single, formless sphere.
An example: enemy soldiers, late
in 1914, carolled each other across the fields.
Could not, next dawn, take up their former places.
Such is the chaos that affection yields.

When did we cut the long-compounded verbs
into their separate nouns,
the worm's life from the bird's?
Must it be loneliness crowns all things
that live? Packed fat of the sea-lion,
fox blood splashing the brush like early sun—
why give them to our wars to be undone?
But what if in truth Love's perfect One were
Dante's sheered disorder, the known world tumbled?
If the longing and stumble of self were made of sin?
Choose Hate, to stay faceted then
in the many and season-stung minds, the battered salmonskin
peeling its sky's flung rind, the blossoming strife.
Choose the cell's dividing, life into life,
the too-bright stream. Choose beauty loved—
how loved—within division's light.

THE WINDOW

I am not—
opened or closed—
what you expected, o heart.

Or would you
without me have thought
to throw open
the flooding and roar,
to step through the lion's gold pelt?

Have thought that
the passionate glass is the body?
And this life, the one life you wanted?

Wanted,
meaning neither *lacked,*
nor *desired,*
but something else.
Something closer
to how, when the two owl-lovers
begin their night singing
and all the black length of the woods
is held in those arms,
not one stone, not one leaf goes uncalling.

If I had been what you thought,
o heart,
how could the clear glass
flow as it does with mountains,
with jewel-colored, perishing fish?
Flashing and falling,
the black-bright rain of beings and things—

Some recognizable, yours, but others—
too fleeting or large—that cannot be spoken.

Though the one world touches the other
in every part, o heart,
in silence,
like new lovers taking their fill in the crowded dark.

THE STONE OF HEAVEN

Here, where the rivers dredge up
the very stone of Heaven, we name its colors—
muttonfat jade, kingfisher jade, jade of appleskin green.

And here, in the glittering
hues of the Flemish Masters, we sample their wine;
rest in their windows' sun-warmth,
cross with pleasure their scrubbed tile floors.
Everywhere the details leap like fish—bright shards
of water out of water, facet-cut, swift-moving
on the myriad bones.

Any woodthrush shows it—he sings,
not to fill the world, but because he is filled.

But the world does not fill with us,
it spills and spills, whirs with owl-wings,
rises, sets, stuns us with planet-rings, stars.
A carnival tent, a fluttering of banners.

O baker of yeast-scented loaves,
sword dancer,
seamstress, weaver of shattering glass,
O whirler of winds, boat-swallower,
germinant seed,
O seasons that sing in our ears in the shape of O—
we name your colors muttonfat, kingfisher, jade,
we name your colors anthracite, orca, growth-tip of pine,
we name them arpeggio, pond,
we name them flickering helix within the cell, burning coal tunnel,
        blossom of salt,

we name them roof flashing copper, frost-scent at morning, smoke-singe
    of pearl,
from black-flowering to light-flowering we name them,
from barest conception, the almost not thought of, to heaviest matter, we
    name them,
from glacier-lit blue to the gold of iguana we name them,
and naming, begin to see,
and seeing, begin to assemble the plain stones of earth.

"Red Poppies": The Lion-Gate Palace was the name of Agamemnon's palace in Greece.

"Each Step": Two sayings lie behind this poem. One is from the Sung Dynasty Chinese Zen master Hsuan-sha (Japanese: Gensha): "All the world is one bright pearl." The other is from the gnostic Gospel of Thomas: "The Kingdom of Heaven is already here on earth, only men do not see."

"The Shadow" is dedicated to Marianne Rey.

"Cycladic Figure: The Harp Player (ca. 3000 B.C.E.)": My thanks to poet Laura Fargas for the gift of a reproduction of this figure.

"History as the Painter Bonnard": My thanks to painter Deborah Kelley for telling me of the artists' term *bonnarding*.

"The Wedding": Lavoisier, considered the father of modern chemistry, proved the law of conservation of matter by separating mercuric oxide into its two component elements—mercury and oxygen—and finding no difference between their combined weight and those of the original and the recombined substances; my thanks to poet and chemist Roald Hoffman for the quotation, which could as easily be a statement of Buddhist teaching.

"Narcissus: Tel Aviv, Baghdad, San Francisco; February 1991": My knowledge of the fact that narcissus were blooming in the Middle East at that time comes from a journal that the Israeli writer Robert Werman was posting to the Internet virtually daily during the Gulf War.

"For the Autumn Dead: Election Day, 1984": The funeral being referred to is Indira Gandhi's. The statistics given are as of that date; for both the Indian riots and the Ethiopian drought, the final estimates are significantly higher.

"Perceptibility Is a Kind of Attentiveness": The translation of this aphorism is John Berger's, from *Ways of Seeing*. The poem speaks to the "ordinary water" of the following passage from the *Shōbōgenzō-Zuimonki* of the Japanese Zen teacher Eihei Dōgen (1200-1253): "There is a place in the ocean where vast waves ceaselessly rise. Without fail, all fish which pass this place become dragons. For that reason, the place is called the Dragon-Gate. The vast waves there are no different from the waves anywhere else, and the water is ordinary salt water as well. Yet mysteriously, all fish crossing here become dragons. Their scales do not change, their bodies do not change, and still they become dragons."

"The Sting": "In one of those/ nine or ten infolded worlds" is a reference to string theory, which posits up to thirteen universes coexisting with the one visible to us.

"This Love": "Paris is missing me" is the literal translation of the French phrasing, *"Paris me manque."*

"Inspiration": A zendo is a meditation hall.

"The Love of Aged Horses": "Chiasmus" is a term from rhetoric, referring to a literary device in which terms are arranged in a crisscrossing pattern.

"The Thief": "For fish, water is endless; for birds, the air" is from the Genjō kōan of Dōgen's *Shōbōgenzō.*

ABOUT THE AUTHOR

Jane Hirshfield is the author of two previous collections of poetry, *Alaya* (1982) and *Of Gravity & Angels* (1988); she is also cotranslator and editor of *The Ink Dark Moon: Love Poems by Ono no Komachi and Izumi Shikibu, Women of the Ancient Court of Japan* (1988; expanded edition 1990) and editor of *Women in Praise of the Sacred: 43 Centuries of Spiritual Poetry by Women* (HarperCollins, 1994). Her work has appeared in many magazines and anthologies, including *The Atlantic Monthly, The Nation, The New Yorker,* the *American Poetry Review, Antaeus, Poetry, Sierra, Yellow Silk,* and the *Paris Review.* She has received a Guggenheim Fellowship in poetry, Columbia University's Translation Center Award, the Commonwealth Club of California's Poetry Medal, and a Pushcart Prize, among other honors. She lives in northern California.

(continued from copyright page)

River Styx: "Narcissus: Tel Aviv, Baghdad, San Francisco; February 1991"; *The Threepenny Review:* "Courtship"; *Upriver/Downriver:* "The Task," "The Stone of Heaven" (reprint); *Volt:* "The Thief"; *Whole Earth Review:* "The Hawk Cry"; *Wilderness:* "For a Wedding on Mount Tamalpais"; *Yellow Silk:* "1973," "The Groundfall Pear," "In Yellow Grass," "Percolation"; *Zyzzyva:* "Meeting the Light Completely," "The Shadow."

"The Stone of Heaven" also appeared in *The 1990 American Poetry Annual* (Roth Publishing Company, 1990). "The Stone of Heaven" and "Inspiration" also appeared in *Beneath a Single Moon: Legacies of Buddhism in Contemporary American Poetry* (Shambhala Publications, 1991). "The Ritual" also appeared in *Earth Against Heaven: A Tiananmen Square Anthology* (Five Islands Press, Australia, 1990). "For the Autumn Dead: Election Day, 1984" first appeared in *Eighty on the Eighties* (Ashland Poetry Press, 1990). "At Nightfall" also appeared in *A Hand-span of Red Earth: An American Farm Poem Anthology* (University of Iowa Press, 1991). "Empedocles' Physics," "Even the Vanishing Housed," "For a Gelding," and "The House in Winter" first appeared in *The Quarterly Review of Literature Fiftieth Anniversary Anthology;* another ten poems were also reprinted there. "Percolation" also appeared in *Sierra: The Magazine of the Sierra Club.* "The Shadow" and "Percolation" also appeared in *Tricycle: The Buddhist Review.* "1973" and "Percolation" also appeared in *The Yellow Silk Anthology* (Crown Publishers, 1990).

I am greatly indebted to the Corporation of Yaddo, the Djerassi Foundation, the Marin Arts Council, and the Dewar's Young Artist Recognition Award Program for their support during the period when many of these poems were written.